FLYING KITES
Friendly Street Poets 36

Judy Dally has published three collections of poetry: *At Sixes and Sevens* (1982), *Holding Up Mirrors* (1983) and *Across the Gulf* (1992). She has also been published in various magazines and newspapers and in the last 23 editions of the Friendly Street Reader. In 2011 she won the John Bray Roman Poetry Prize with *Whoever Said of Shane Warne*.

In 1994 she completed a Master of Arts in Literature from Deakin University. She tutored in Australian Literature and Adolescent Fiction at the University of SA Magill in 1992 and was a primary school teacher for 22 years. She is currently a member of the Tutti Choir and a volunteer teaching literacy at Tutti Arts (young people with a disability studying art, music and drama).

Judy lives in glorious semi-retirement at Glenelg with her husband John (who is also a great proof-reader!) and enjoys reading, live theatre, sailing and socialising.

Louise McKenna was born in the United Kingdom where she studied at the University of Nottingham and the University of Leeds, graduating with a Joint Honours degree in English and French. She lived for a short spell in France and New Zealand before making Australia her permanent home in 2003.

Louise was a finalist in the inaugural Cricket Poetry Award 2009. Her first collection of poetry, *A Lesson in Being Mortal*, was published in *Friendly Street New Poets 15* by Wakefield Press in 2010. Her work has since appeared in *Sorcerers and Soothsayers: Friendly Street Poets 35*, *The Independent Weekly*, *Poetrix* and *paper wasp*. She has read some of her poetry on Radio Adelaide and recently won Poem of the Month in the monthly science poem competition held by the Royal Institute of Australia. Louise works part time as a Registered Nurse. She is married to Dave and has two sons.

FLYING KITES

Friendly Street Poets 36

Edited by

Judy Dally and Louise McKenna

§

Friendly Street Poets

Friendly Street Poets Incorporated
PO Box 3697
Norwood
South Australia 5067
friendlystreetpoets.org.au

Wakefield Press
1 The Parade West
Kent Town
South Australia 5067
wakefieldpress.com.au

First published 2012

Cover artwork by Judy Garrard
Designed and typeset by Clinton Ellicott, Wakefield Press
Edited by Judy Dally and Louise McKenna, Friendly Street Poets Inc.
Printed in Australia by Griffin Digital, Adelaide

ISBN 978 1 74305 100 9

Government
of South Australia

Arts SA

Friendly Street Poets Inc. is supported
by the **South Australian Government**
through **Arts SA**.

CONTENTS

THANK YOU

to the poets who read at the city and regional meetings
and submitted their work for this book
and to the supportive and appreciative audiences.

Our thanks also to Arts SA for their continuing support,
which keeps our publishing program financially viable.

Special thanks to Judy Garrard for her beautiful
cover artwork.

Thanks also to John Pfitzner and John Dally for their
generous assistance with proofreading.

ACKNOWLEDGEMENT

Friendly Street Poets acknowledges the Kaurna people
as the original owners and custodians of the Adelaide Plains.

PREFACE

In the middle of the night
We keep sending little kites
Until a little light gets through
        (Patty Griffin 'Kite Song')

In some ways our poems are our kites. We write them and
we fly them in the public sky so that people can admire their
beauty and their grace. They are a message to all who care
to look up and read them. Some of them fly easily and carry
on the wind. Some of them flop and fall to the ground.

When a poem lifts and sustains flight, it is an exhilarating
experience. The poems we have selected from the eight
hundred and fifty poems submitted for this anthology are
kites that risked exposure before audiences at a variety of
locations. The conditions were right. The poems soared and
their flight endured. They are beautiful enough to catch the
eye, buoyant enough to fly free on their own and interesting
enough to make a lasting impression.

Among the voices published here are many new poets
who have never previously weathered the experience of
publication. Mentored poets and recipients of Friendly Street
prizes are also included. We hope you enjoy this collection,
and revel in the aerial dynamics of the poetry.

Judy Dally and Louise McKenna

OLD COUPLE

Velvet fingers, subtle in cheeky caress
As if no one is watching
A wink scatters butterflies in both;
Tonight will be electric
A glass of Italy voids inhibition
All walls are down
Who needed them anyway?
His eyes are twinkling
Her words as smooth as the oysters

And their felicity makes my youthful love look like child's play
I know this is more than a fool's night;
There is a ring on his finger
As on hers
It's been forty years
And he's never felt more alive

TADRO ABBOTT

BELL HOUR

And you

my bell jar
my hour glass

more than jar and glass
my bell hour

such curved
bellness

so fertile lush
so woman

so blooming
almost mother

you toll for me
your belly's toll

you peal, you chime
this is your hour

the future
courses through

and you
and you

and me
and three

of us

DAVID ADÈS
Poem of the Month, February 2011

THINGS I MUST DO

Before I eat, I must know hunger –
the hollow resonance of an emptied vessel, a litany of absences.

Before I drink, I must know thirst –
desert grit lining mouth and throat, dry tongue restless.

Before I judge, I must suspend judgement –
hold it high over cliff's edge, above the thunder of rocks.

Before I take offence, I must open windows –
let fresh air into all the musty rooms of my house.

Before I love, I must lie naked with loneliness –
run hands over its body, touch its moist and intimate secrets.

Before I die, I must take one pure breath –
without fear, without lust, without bitterness.

DAVID ADÈS

COMING UP FOR AIR

Fear keeps her there,
drives her out for empty hours,
brings her creeping back
to stand motionless
at the kitchen bench, lie rigid,
cold under the covers in the afternoon.

Fear teaches her to lie
but doesn't buy peace.
The futility of pretence stings,
sometimes leaves a mark.
A partly open door admits a sigh,
slams into silence. Heavy footfall
down the hall says all it wants her to hear.

Fear pulls her down
when she comes up for air,
leaves her limp and breathless,
spilling her guts to strangers.
Courage comes with a question,
its answer stowed safely in her suitcase
as she leaves.

KATE ALDER

AMAZING GRACE DEC 10
– HAIKU SEQUENCE

courtyard ensemble
a jingle of carols
herald an event

in her black hair
a red poinsettia
keeps the beat

flake of colour
this red bark
carries the tune

his red tie
matches her flower
harmony of voice

callistemon
in a flourish of scarlet
finishes the score

summer courtyard
in a festive mood
an amazing grace

MAEVE ARCHIBALD

A DAY IN ROME – HAIKU SEQUENCE

lapis lazuli sky
   over the Vatican
     a dove

ancient cobbles
tattoo of surprise
Roman Street

slice of pizza
a wedge of history
   the topping

    side by side
past and present
Piazza Navonna

blood oranges
Spanish Steps
   at sunset

underlit
   the river
     by night

MAEVE ARCHIBALD

EYELASHES

You have a tendency,
eyes half closed,
to let your eyelashes entice
and make me prisoner.
But sometimes their slim fixtures
are iron bars across a window
and lock me out.

You have a tendency,
your eyes wide-open, to surprise
innocently, by ambush,
unexpectedly swallowing
where I am
with bright lights
and prickling stars.

You have a tendency
to seek me out
when I look into the sky
and employ strange creatures
to crowd about my eyes' edges
and order me to swim
against the currents of my heart.

HENRY ASHLEY-BROWN

TRICKSTER

The hare with quiet gaze
holds the valley still
and its silence is the iris
of the lidded frost-white hill

Listening, long-eared, erect
it keeps time's dance suspended
and the kiss of the moon-mirrored sun
and the songs of stars that have ended

Here is a place of grey shadows
and emptiness full of dreams
sun that conspires with moonlight
and where nothing is as it seems

This is the threshold of being
that the warm-eyed hare keeps still
for the old gods and the new gods
and the travellers who cross the hill.

Temples and churches and highways
lie beneath the frost-pillowed grass
where the hare and the hill watch us
in silence as we pass.

HENRY ASHLEY-BROWN

NOCTURNE IN DOWNTOWN FLAT

Nightfall over the banging traffic
an elephant-trunk pours grey
smoke from a chimney-stack
making a falling column
over the darkening trees
and spider-leg Dali-dreams

and some siren wails
for the sky is a pull-down blind
streetlights blink awake
washed with orange
and a vodka bridge
rolls past on
banging metal feet.

there's a blunder of thunder
and flights
of traffic lights,
this dance is for diesel
electric spiderwebs
and long-range impressions

of solitary windows
lit up with
tables and chairs still awake long
long past midnight
and the tearaway clouds
are rabbits
in their bolt-holes.

aah the rain weeps silver
the rain weeps gold,
and now that the night is laughing
fit to bust as it
announces the next stop:

all the train-tracks run
to the crescendo moon
and now, now
they hit the night
like an anvil of stars!

AVALANCHE

PLAYING TRUANT

It must have been the morning breeze
and the rusty red whiliwinds of dust
that pulled him from the road
and enticed him into the bush,
his country ripe with sunlight
and patchily shadowed with gums.
Shoes in hand, he wanders at will,
counting the goannas he can see
and those he senses along the track.
He marks the line of a fallen tree,
carries that angle in his head.
Miss would have given him an early minute.
Only a minute? He's taking a day.
For lunch, dry biscuits and a slab of cheese
but later he'll seek out
tart purple berries to sweeten it.
With time to story the landscape
he watches the way great clouds
lazily sail across the sky.
Despite the drift of the afternoon
he guesses the time to make for home.
Back on the road he measures his steps,
chanting some words to match the rhythm
of his sandals slapping against the bitumen.

ELAINE BARKER

BESIDE THE RIVER

Somewhere in your mind you find a place
to accommodate this trail of shoes –
a bronze installation and a likeness
of the shabby footwear
worn by the women and children
forced into lines along the embankment
on those ghost days beside the Danube
when the winter was iron
and the wind cut cruelly as a bayonet.
The river was the colour of want,
dark and deep-flowing,
ready to seize and carry away
the victims in its undertow,
and silently
when there should have been singing.
So you take in this low-lying row of shoes,
hear the shots,
the cascading splash,
try to imagine the watery journey
of souls whose absence
even now unsettles the air.
Starlings have no such memory though
as they fidget and flutter their way
between the shoes and over the cobblestones.

*The plaque beside this memorial on the bank of the Danube in Budapest
reads: In memory of the victims shot into the Danube by Arrow Cross
militiamen in 1944–45.*

ELAINE BARKER

FISHERMAN'S LIFE, FISHERMAN'S WIFE

Fishing sounded good, so clean I thought
simple and sanctioned, an air about it;
Those souls who cast their nets at first light,
in plain boats, weren't they the very salt.

It was diesel, grease, pubs and yarns, it was
dragging the ocean floor; the odd Flat
caught among the shells – a silver prize
delivered, with the smile of a cat.

We watched you leave the wharf, the child and I,
all three of us in moonlight, the sea singing
with it, you did the ropes like fisherman's Tai
Chi, and were gone like an eel swimming.

KAREN BLAYLOCK

A LESSON IN MATH

I was helping my daughter
solve a math problem
& it went
something like this

*The entire populations
of two towns are to
attend a meeting together
there are 340 people
in one town
& 671 in another,
how many chairs
will be needed?*

I told her
this is the kind
of thing
Dad does at work

& suggested
she picture in her head
having to arrange
such a meeting

Suddenly she said
*I've got it! It just came to me,
you add them up!*

Very good
I said
*did it help
to imagine
the situation?*

Not really
she replied
I could just see in my head
a cleaner
moving chairs
around a big hall
& someone else
was there
with a pen & paper
working it all out

She's going
straight to the top.

STEVE BROCK
Read at RiAus, August 2011

OF A HAIKU-SIZED PERSON

moment
by moment
her first day

grasping my finger
a tiny perfect
newborn hand

dusk light
a tear on the cheek
of the baby

on the baby's belly
a tenderness
of hands

blissful
in the arms of her mother
the tiny sleeping face

BELINDA BROUGHTON

DOVES

Where the horse manure,
rank and steaming, melted the snow

doves would come on their thin feet
to peck at the undigested grain.

I understand how they came
to be a symbol of peace

with their domestic colours
and soft voices

how they love
with such devotion

how watching them
can soothe a war-torn heart.

I threw fresh seed or crumbled bread
and they came pecking

and crooning their one soft syllable
hoo, hoo

the sort of sound one makes for a lover
or whispers into a baby's ear.

BELINDA BROUGHTON

AMERICA

the seven wonders of the world
can be found
on the Great Plains of America

they successfully quashed
the underground
on the remote island that is America

you blacks, you Jews
you peace-loving hippies
from setting sun America

the great woods
keep falling
for parking-lot America

and the Angels
are calling out
for the old & true America

San Francisco fell
long ago
to the woe that fills America

and with Greenwich Village
buried under the snow
I smell death on you America

your short history
is full of tears
my bleeding heart America

TED

rica

America?

thousand men

America

sand

itch America

rner of the world
to grow
ow of America

OPHER BRUNNER

YOUNG MAN'S DEATH REVISIT

with apologies to Roger McGough

Let me die a young man's death.
Not a Dworkin assisted,
plastic bag,
out of breath death.

When I'm 73,
on my way to the hearing aid shop,
let me be run down by a green Prius driven by Pink.
Whisper quiet, she'd text me to get out of the way
but I wouldn't hear it over my iPod.

Or when I'm 91,
let me die in a hail of bullets
in an airport lounge,
after my hip replacement sets off the metal detector
and the security guards don't appreciate my sense of humour

Or when I'm 104,
let me suffer cybersex electrocution,
after an explosive conjunction of AC and DC
in my web-connected Loving Machine.

Oh, let me die a young man's death.
Not a politically correct,
low fat, high fibre,
"It was in his genes" death.

JOHN BRYDON
Poem of the Month, July 2011

but you got rid
of all your fears
didn't you? Iron Fist America

strong and free
master of all
do you love yourself America?

for a few thousand men
your enemies fall
rattle your sabre America

the blood in the sand
ebbs and flows
for the Angel-Bitch America

and in my corner of the world
it's so hard to grow
in the shadow of America

CHRISTOPHER BRUNNER

YOUNG MAN'S DEATH REVISITED

with apologies to Roger McGough

Let me die a young man's death.
Not a Dworkin assisted,
plastic bag,
out of breath death.

When I'm 73,
on my way to the hearing aid shop,
let me be run down by a green Prius driven by Pink.
Whisper quiet, she'd text me to get out of the way
but I wouldn't hear it over my iPod.

Or when I'm 91,
let me die in a hail of bullets
in an airport lounge,
after my hip replacement sets off the metal detector
and the security guards don't appreciate my sense of humour.

Or when I'm 104,
let me suffer cybersex electrocution,
after an explosive conjunction of AC and DC
in my web-connected Loving Machine.

Oh, let me die a young man's death.
Not a politically correct,
low fat, high fibre,
"It was in his genes" death.

JOHN BRYDON
Poem of the Month, July 2011

MY FINEST HOUR

I ease my Triumph Spitfire into a shallow dive
with the parking spot dead ahead.
The radio crackles,
Bandits at niner zero.

I catch sight of a VW who hasn't yet seen me.
I turn towards him, but then as my mirror shatters
I see a Beemer banking hard behind me, gun ports sparkling.
The old out of the sun trick.

I side slip then throw an Immelman.
We pass nose to nose so close I can see his eyes.

By chance we both break right
slap into the Volvo that neither of us saw coming.
Stooging around as a non-combatant
but still managing to get in the way.

Hanging from our chutes
we mentally compose our respective insurance reports.
The camaraderie of war ensuring that we will
both blame the Volvo
and keep our no-claims bonuses intact.

JOHN BRYDON

ILLUSIONS OF EXISTENCE

We sail on the waves
of a particle sea,
mathematical shadows.

Here thing and nothing
lose their contradiction
and dance a Heisenberg waltz,
the uncertainty of all we know as certain
masked.

Atoms
each a tree falling in the forest of matter
non reality
surges of probability, endlessly rolling
not yet knowing their time and space

until
sentient glance reveals
something resembling
the illusions of our existence.

DAVID CALE
Read at RiAus, August 2011

SAILING THE TECTONIC SEAS

The mountain rears magnificent
a titanic ship's prow
cuts through countless dawns
sun-warmed, storm wracked
mute testimony
to tectonic brooding
of the planet below our feet

I am tempted to feel small

But a mountain is just a mountain
not a comment on me

DAVID CALE
Read at RiAus, August 2011

THE KITE

Its rustle sound manoeuvres
fooling a homebound gull;
wheeling and soaring
like a large colourful eagle hawk.

MARTIN CHRISTMAS

HUNTER GATHERER

I took your land
and gave you tea and sugar.
I took your hunting
and gave you bags of flour.

I brought my God
and laughed at the Guditja
Scoffed at pitjiri
and gave you wine.

Your feet that trod the land
have nowhere else to go

You hunt and gather now
the only way you can.
Your hand, that held the spear
outstretched and waiting.

MARGARET CLARK

NIGHT IN THE SUBURBS

After the chattering families have slipped behind curtains,
and dark cars,   wetly returning,   have swooped into driveways;
doors slam,   lights shut,   and   tight footsteps crunch into silence;
the dogs stop yapping, and nothing's more   single,   alone,   than
street lights on watch exposing a desert of streets and
quenching the stars

I am threatened by fences:
I am afraid of prim hedges and walls which are always   separate.

Silent suburbs turn their backs on you.

In the country you can step out into eternity
and shelter under a friendly canopy of air.

BETTY COLLINS

DEEPWATER BLOBFISH

Psychrolutes marcidus

I would not like my name
if I were capable of knowing.
I am all gelatinous body,
colourless, or you could say pink-white
as though drained of blood and life,
but alive, flopped like mucoid detritus
on the ocean's bed.

My squint eyes form a half smile
as my prey presses close
to my blubbery mouth.
I have no muscles.
My languorous lips open
for lobster or bottom feeding fish
and I imbibe.

There must be more to life
than these black depths,
more than intake and excretion.
Ah, if I have a heart
I cannot speak of it breaking.
It melts constantly
with yearning.

DAWN COLSEY
Mentored Poet 2011
Poem of the Month, August 2011

TANKA

A child's white kite
flying against black sky?
raucous screeching
cockatoo, wings spread wide
wind buffeted

DAWN COLSEY
Mentored Poet 2011

CHINATOWN MARKET

Inscrutable
   this Oriental seer
with bamboo pole
       twice his height
juggles a paper lantern
toward the rail far above
     to hang there
among the cobwebs
       like a last peach.
Hand over hand
   it teeters higher
      ever higher –
all but
   slips
      plummets.

With a cymbal clash of obscenity
    he derides himself
         looks up
   sees me watching
     so must turn away
to retrieve more than his mask
   before he may try again.

DAVID COOKSON
Read at Seaford, July 2011

FISHER

He is a world of winds
and tides; a narrowness
grafted to the rail
just left of the bollard,
by a certain whiff
of aged bait.
A roll-your-own
imperils a week's beard
as he sucks in its smoke,
casts one-handed
twenty metres clear
of the jetty.
A finger cracked
as an old strap
snags the line
to translate any nudge
from the mystery below,
as he waits, monosyllabic
with even his peers,
not caring to share the lore;
less, his own ebb and flow.

DAVID COOKSON
Read at Seaford, July 2011

HEATWAVE

When bad light stops play at beach cricket
and dogs are too tired to chase balls,
after sandcastles are flattened
and children's squeals silent
a bonfire sun sizzles into the sea
as technicolour shelters are packed away.

Once the car-park empties
of salt-pickled bodies and boogie-boards,
the beach is ours, to pick up plastic bags,
broken yellow spades and empty coke cans
discarded like yesterday's promises,
relish the quiet, brief rulers of our realm.

For tomorrow's another scorcher –
like a plague, the mob will return.

VERONICA COOKSON
Read at Seaford, July 2011

AUTUMN IN COLLINS STREET

Plane trees cast off
brown paper cut outs
leaves that swirl
around boots and high heels
in black suits and tan
faces stare ahead
no time to stop.

Plane trees let loose
over-sized moths
leaves that flutter
around lace-ups and courts
in navy suits and grey
mobiles to ears
no time to waste.

Plane trees moult
a monochrome mosaic
leaves in decay
while Brack's sepia crowds
scuttle past in endless waves
going nowhere and everywhere
determined to get there soon.

VERONICA COOKSON
Read at Seaford, July 2011

NIGHT TERRORS

Sweat soaks
my childhood-summer-holiday sheets
in this black-sand-surrounded
holiday shanty
three miles from the sea.

No light shines
through my window
and the spiders
which have hidden
from the light
all day in cracks
between asbestos sheets
and wooden joists
roister now
across my bedroom ceiling.

I have islanded
my bed
away from walls
and window frames
but I can hear
their conspiratorial whispers
feel the feathered edges
of their webs
against my face.

And in the darkness
my skin feels them
crawling
wall to wall
as they watch me
seem to sleep.

Across the room
my brother snores, oblivious,
dreaming blue-sea-sun-gold
visions of the day
untroubled by
non-existent spiders.

JUDY DALLY

I CAN'T WRITE LETTERS

I write leaves
In the sky
Water
In the wind
And you do read
What I write
You read with your skin

JELENA DINIC
Mentored poet 2011

DEAR WORDS

Please
find heart in your letters
to forgive me.
Find forgiveness in your meanings
that I borrow without asking.

I trap you in a poem
like amber spiders in its light
transparent
helpless
beautiful inside.

I line you up
you precious words
and you follow each other blind.
Wisdom grows
as I steal your secrets
between the lines.

And one day,
when I take you all where the page ends
and when I close my eyes with content
you will, my hand made art,
come back to me all
off by heart.

JELENA DINIC
Mentored poet 2011
Poem of the Month, June 2011

FISH

Behind the glass
      a surgical display, bright
flesh like gems
      pearlescent pinks
and moonstone white,
      amethyst tangled tentacles
with multicoloured mounds of marinara
a pornography of wetted filets.

Red snapper's stoic jaw,
      butterfish like silver bullets
   yellow-back of salmon-trout,
mackerel's regimental stripes,
and fryingpan snappers' moonlight bodies,
salmon heads,
fins like sharp edged shadows,
and all those vivid eyes
      wide-black
for the shame of sudden death.

This beauty is too intimate.

JO DEY

A GREEN SEA

A green sea runs before the wind,
conveying silver light, a molten thing,
back towards the sun.

The brilliance mounts in drifts
on wavelets stretching to
the horizon's white abyss,
unfathomable receiver of the light.

Two kite-boards out there now,
under blue crescents,
are riding what they cannot catch.

Breaking ripples smear the sand with platinum
and the white of it might carry us
into that restless radiance,
the ever-moving masquerade of water.

JO DEY

SHEDS

Old shed leans on barbered paddock
its bleaching sheets of iron flap like rusted hope,
wind whips along barbed wire
mocking flood and drought and plague.

He brushes flies, flips a bushie's hat,
heaves his tired body from the ute
back sore, nails broken, black hair
thick with dust, boots scuffed and cracked.

The fertile promise of the land
knot his past, present and old age.
It is what he knows and all he wants to know
reflecting in a corrugated face.

There is comfort in the shed,
its weathered shelter of shared memories
a place to release hot tears
his roars of disappointed rage.
In secret.

TESS DRIVER

WRITING MARTIN

for Martin

I write your name
on window panes

I clap out its five syllables
for the five fingers of my hand

and the five senses
lost and abandoned

I see deep white snow
and signposts buried in the drifts

I hear the jet black engine
running under my sternum

I touch the mirrored stillness
You still, me still here

I smell the red raw emptiness
bloodied, boned and free

I taste the green of bitterness acid
etching ulcers in a tender stomach wall

I trace the ink of your signature
follow each loop and dot of the 'i'

that 'i' Martin
that has been erased forever.

M.L. EMMETT

BAVARIAN AUNT

Aunt Lottie had a slow and careful walk
every step could jar
the delicate balance
of the fragile grand piano
she had swallowed.

It was no ordinary instrument
it was entirely made of crystal
which added to the fears
of its disturbance
or destruction
by the simplest slip or stumble
or missed footing on a step.

It was a slight inconvenience
she had taken in her stride.
Matters concerning the said piano
were only discussed in hushed tones
on Wednesday afternoons
and only with her dearest nephew, Ludwig,
who sensitively seemed to understand
the precious nature of imagination
and the tickling discomforts
of digested furniture and such things
as fancy may create.

M.L. EMMETT

ELLY AT ELEVEN

She is feathers whispering on the eye
of summer dawn. She is bubbles born
on the glitter of champagne. She is a gazelle
her legs longer than a flamingo's.
She is a memory of fairy pink: her reflection
blurs in still water. She is a marionette
who trusts she'll be held by the sky.

SUSAN FEALY

JULY MORNING

On this not-quite-frost morning
the native lilac
sprinkles its purple blooms
on the dry brush fence
plane tree leaves lie like cut-out paper stars
the sparse blades
of kangaroo grass are green in the sun
and plant shadows patch
the would-be lawn
recalling
black shadow lattice of the vine
bare in the full moon.

MARGARET FENSOM

VENUS

The deadly beauty of the planet Venus
White lily in twilight's garden
Tells us perhaps that dreams
Are best glimpsed from afar.
For there are fiery beauties in the skies
Too fierce for human flesh
But wonderful no less.

MARGARET FENSOM

SYNAPSES

sometimes
it is possible
to lift the rusted catch
of the skylight, creak it out
into blue air
stand there
breathing in
the wind's chemistry
with the knowledge that
somebody I don't know
who lives in a
different country
is also standing
in a room
in their house
with the window open
looking   out
and   up
at a sky that might be
dark and star punched
or stretched wide with sunshine
or clouded and closed
but is still

essentially

the same sky
that is outside
my open window

ALISON FLETT
Poem of the Month, May 2011

THE CHECHEN SMILE

Into the languishing light
she steps outside,
greeted by a hollow sun,
further darkening the decaying buildings.

Shadows of grey illuminate injured edifices,
death's lurid painting: a dirty mess of black and white
thrown on a pristine canvas.
She makes her way, resigned.

A world raided of beauty,
devoid of colour, drenched in devastation
stagnant save for a cock,
that slowly pecks his way around her blistered feet.

A flash of colour shrouds her weary body.
A floral dress,
whispering hope in the faded folds of fabric
mocks the possibility.

The water trickles pitifully into her bucket,
each drop like a sharp mirror
reflecting her indigent image,
her weary world.

She treads the streets guardedly cradling the bucket,
that not a single drop should fall,
passing mournful mounds of rubble
where once homes stood.

Yet she smiles for the photo
and continues on her way,
escorted by the menacing roar of engines overhead –
a relentless reminder of those who are dead.

KATARINA FOLEY
(age 17 years)
First Prize in the Friendly Street section of 2011 Spring Poetry Festival

MY FATHER

My father has
Wavy hair
Clean skin
And immaculate taste in clothes

We are very different men

He hates our differences

He complains about my crew-cuts
He hates crew-cuts

He complains about my goatie beards
He hates goatie beards

He complains about my tattoos
He hates tattoos

He complains about my jeans and t-shirts
He hates jeans and t-shirts

He complains about my thongs
He hates thongs

But
I am my father's son
And every morning
I shave his face
In my mirror

He hates seeing his face
With my crew-cuts and goatie beards
He hates seeing his body
With my tattoos, my jeans and t-shirts and my thongs

He doesn't hate me
He hates our similarities

And he thinks his complaints will change me
But he won't win
I won't let him

I am my own man
Not my old man

And he really hates that.

NIGEL FORD
Read at Salisbury, August 2011

LINGUA FRANCA

Love me in English
& I'll make you tea and muffins
Soak you in, sip you up

Love me in *po-Russki*
& I'll make you bortsch
Drink your blood, red hot

Love me in *Espanol*
& I'll cook chilli con carne
Spice you up, scream you down

Love me in *Italiano*
& I'll make spaghetti al dente
Tie you up, bite right through

Love me *en Français*
& I'll serve pâté and wine
Smear you up, wash you down

Love me *b'Ivrit*
& I'll make you falafel
Wrap you up, fill you in

Love me in utter silence
& I'll make you tongue casserole
chat you up, lick you down

Love me in Lingua Franca
Leave me speechless
& hunger we shall not.

DESIREE S. GEZENTSVEY

AN OCEAN BETWEEN US

Remind the wind
to bring your scent to me

Remind the sun
to tell you about my day

Remind the moon
to tell me about your night

Remind me why
we don't see the same sky

One day ahead
One day behind

Remind me why

DESIREE S. GEZENTSVEY

SOMETIMES IT HURTS

When you come to me
I feel your heat before your touch,
I feel the wind, hot, from a mid-summer
night, prickling with dried leaves,
endlessly irritable crickets, incipient thirst,
with the inevitable sunrise that follows,
that, in this climate of ill-defined seasons,
threatens fire before our first morning breath.

When you come to me,
I shiver like a violin string;
in cold sweat, my lip glistens with
dew-drops, my skin draws tight, tighter,
constricts my arteries and veins, a thunderbolt
blinds my shadows, ghostly spectres haunt
my path, sing storm-wracked sirens' songs,
disguise ancient fog-bound shipping hazards.

When you come to me,
I count all the stars across the sky,
the sandgrains on the beach, in the desert,
the heartbeats I always lose, the pangs
I fear as your caresses slip unguided
into the voids of boundless space, as each
and every one of your kisses falls into
unacknowledged whispers around me.

*Most women experience genital pain at some time in their lives, but for
surprisingly many, it is always there.*

IAN GIBBINS

SPARROW TAKES A CHANCE AT THE ART GALLERY CAFÉ

Hey, Sparrow! If I were you, I wouldn't hang
    around here after breadcrumbs,
not with all this passionfruit, organic yoghurt,
    this rich mountain-roast coffee,
infused with spices far too exotic for those of us
    bred from simple earth and
uncluttered air, for those of us who call home
    nests surreptitiously woven
from discards of lavishly curated gardens and
    sheer mirror-glass office blocks.

So keep your eyes open, Sparrow! You have
    the prerequisite skill. Of course,
it's in your blood, your immigrant genetic code,
    evolving one year to the next,
while we meander along, bigger than our boots,
    tripping over naming protocols,
deeds of possession, entitlements under law,
    markets that rise and falter like
old-fashioned radios seeking bandwidth
    in short-wave temptations of desire.

Who knows, Sparrow, you might get lucky!
    There's always the bruschetta.
And no-one is looking. No-one will ever notice
    should a portion take flight,
accompany you down the lane, if a small piece
    should drop from your grasp,
disturb a dreamer below, beg the time of day or night,
    recall a distant harbour,
fish gone missing, gulls and cormorants heading
    resolute, resigned, inland.

You'd best be off now, Sparrow! We both should depart.
    The doors and windows
must close soon, as canvases relax a little, as mitres
    and hard-edged mattes soften
around memory and premonition, as if we guess
    the futures they circumscribe,
the wing-beats they eventually will entrap, between
    the lightness of your touch
and the dead-weight of mine, amongst the inter-leaves
    of our scraggy family trees.

IAN GIBBINS

LOVE POEM

When I die
And go to hell
Promise me
You'll come as well.

PETER GOLDSWORTHY

DANCE OF AUTUMN

The Japanese maple
wears her best skirt
of burnt orange.
The hem dips fashionably
swaying to the rhythm
of autumn breezes.
Red and golden leaves
flutter from her moving limbs
as she starts her dance into winter.

JILL GOWER

OUT OF SEASON

The tide is up
on Brighton beach

waves power
against the sea wall

& from the café window
we watch

a man saunters
along the jetty

weather-beaten face
grey hair

he falters
& pulls on a yellow swim cap

descends steps
to brave the chill of autumn water

once again becomes
the iron man he used to be

JILL GOWER

BLUE RINGED OCTOPUS

In a moon silvered pool
behind a shell
and dancing ripple
a little angel
with dreamy kiss
pulsing electric blue

slipping under
a leafy edge
her watery garden
softly lit
by each heavenly beat
a beauty that leaves me
lost for words –

SIMON HANSON

LIMESTONE

Our house is made from sea shells
coral and the bones of fish
pressed in these blocks of stone
once the bed of an ancient sea
their remains laid to rest
in this house last night
I dreamt of Silurian seas alive
turquoise waters and colourful fish
plankton and coral reefs
life teeming in its trillions
one by one they fell
onto the sea floor
in these stones brimming of the past
so many stories cradled within
stories in want of telling
and with the fall of the night
on the shores of sleep
adrift among these stories
I wonder if these stones
might whisper to me again tonight.

SIMON HANSON

BANGING FOR THE AULD TRIANGLE CROWD

Excellent news
if you are reading this in Yatala
not for you – the inmate – so much as myself
the poet.
I feel that a prison audience
would allow me some valuable street cred
among all the other poets
who are, let's face it, mostly small-handed dandies
and women who believed in unicorns
and wore purple crushed velvet
when they were girls.
If, however, you – the inmate –
are a rock spider from B-Division
or doer of white collar crimes
please pass this on to someone else
smuggled in a Gideon's Bible
or wrapped 'round a shank handle
stuck into some junkie recidivist
who owes you a pack of White Ox.
So eventually it is read
by a true blue collar bloke
down on his luck
fell in with the wrong crowd
made some bad life choices
who regularly
phones Three D's Prison Show
giving shout outs
to his missus on the outside
and requesting AC/DC's Jailbreak
for all his mates in F-Division
and who will go back to roofing
if he gets good behaviour in July.

ROB HARDY

PETALS

for Helen

maybe it takes something
the death of a father
to get a handful of children
onto an out of season beach to scatter petals
in the shallows which roll around their limbs
prickling needle points of cold
under a blank sky
while their parents punch out & punch through
their eyes pinched against the wind
& the ashes

RORY HARRIS

FLAT

wide flat & wild
a wind ruffling an horizon

a mother's wand of hand
over a fresh hair cut son

RORY HARRIS

EYES

where to
put your

hands around
a cup

of tears
your eyes

stare past
the coffin

turning back
on yourself

looking
both ways

RORY HARRIS

LAST OF THE CAT POEMS

Please, not another cat poem
no more couplets for cuddly companions
unless to recount the leftover birds which litter the lawn
whilst puss sits inside with blood on his claws
and purrs satisfaction.

I plead with you desist from that paean to pussy palship
save to summon up that stench in the yard
which neighborhood moggies love to bombard
with tom spray and cat shit.

I beg of you no more veneration of feline affection
but to catalogue each Australian creature
which through cat predation wobbles and teeters
on the edge of extinction.

I implore you, no more tributes to Tabby Tom and Persian Cleo
except to decry the midnight caterwauling
the screeches, the wails, the quarrels appalling
below my bedroom window.

Not more TS Eliot-like whimsical narration
unless to promote the wearing of flat cat hats
with fur flaps and tails which help to combat
the proliferating pussy population.

No, no not even a moggie haiku
until we bid the last cat in Australia farewell
with a tolling not a tinkling bell
a ding dong dell
an obituary, a eulogy, a remembrance will do.

MIKE HOPKINS
Poem of the Month, December 2010

THE ADELAIDE TAXI DRIVER'S PRAYER

after Ian Dury

Our cabfare, which starts in Cavan
Hallett Cove be thy aim
Thy Kingswood come
Thy Willaston
In Hove as it is in Hendon
Give us Largs Bay and Birkenhead
And forgive us our Crafers West
As we forgive those that Crafers against us
And lead us not into Keswick Station
But deliver us from Frewville
For thine is the Findon
The Paralowie and the Salisbury
Rostrevor, Rostrevor
Mile End.

MIKE HOPKINS

THIS POEM

this poem is rainbow daggers not barrels of gold
this poem is pointing in your face like a gun of light
this poem is light
       and heavy at the same time
this poem is a big blank page
         is your pen writing without the guidance of your fingertips
this poem is a line of people standing for miles so nobody can tell
   with their eyes
that the line curves ever so slightly and meets back up with itself
this poem is itself
       it is not ham or cheese
       blue eggs and cauliflower
            peas sitting on a plate uneaten
this poem is to be digested over a long time having been peppered
   by the fingers of each soul standing in that curving line
this poem just is
       it is understated and would not read itself
this poem is forgotten
       finished, done

this poem is undone
this poem is a rolling saga
this poem is too long for you to listen to
       too long to start

but this poem is started
       and finished in one sentence
this poem is a repetition of one sentence
this poem is a repetition of one sentence
this poem says one thing over and over and
       over and over and over and over and over
and this poem is not over
this poem is an infinite string of words
       wound like a spider spool into an infinitely long ball of thread
this poem is a cat with the thread
       of infinity stuck between its claws
this poem is your finite life reading to itself
       from a piece of paper that may not even exist
this poem is small, it is a piece
       a small piece of life
       a small piece of paper caught by the wind whispering its
  secrets to the sky
this poem is rainbow daggers not barrels of gold
this poem is a rolling saga
       too long for you to listen
       too round to start
       or finish
this poem is about to become invisible
this poem will continue writing itself unseen
       over and over and
          over and over and
             over ... and ...

INDIGO

SHE BESPOKE ME

after a poetry reading by Tessa Leon

She spoke to me of dreams
and stars, those liquorice allsorts
hanging from fruit loops in the sky.
She was magic on stage,
all upright, tall as the dark sky,
illuminating the whole room as
if it were a black hole and she
were the origin of the universe.

She spoke of journeys, expeditions,
encounters and I encountered
something in her words,
stopped counting seconds and
started to become,
mesmerised by the unpacking of clouds
from her bag.
And how many rainbows did
she have hidden in her throat?

It was hard to tell in the
dreamy state she swung us in
but I did find out one important
and solid fact, that the number two
is really an immature seven
or a 12 in disguise,
cloaked in invisibility from the cruelness
and crisp cold of the world.

Citizen of that place of rainbows
and lollipops
she spoke and we listened
silent as the stars being read
a bedtime fable.

INDIGO

I THOUGHT THE MOON WAS A COP CAR IN MY REAR VISION MIRROR AS I DROVE HOME LATE LAST NIGHT

… appearing as it did   suddenly
seemingly just over my shoulder
startling
   with blinding highbeam brightness

so i did the only obvious thing
i could think of
in my sleep-deprived somnia

i tried to outrun it –
– outgun it by shifting into fifth
– swerving into corners
– recklessly crossing double lines trying to cut loose
   the antishadow   seeking to bust me
   for misdemeanors real or imagined
– tyres squealing like sirens desperately clingsticking
   to the too tight curves
– brake pads burning away
   via my adrenalin-induced tension

occasionally i thought i'd got away
only for the light to reappear
howling through the trees
a law-enforcing banshee
close as before
   maybe closer

it took maybe 8, 9 minutes   perhaps 12, 13 k's
to realise my pursuer
was no officer of the constabulary
but a humble satellite
doing its nightly security patrol
across the countryside sky

i pulled off the highway
into a parking bay to
   consider my insane behavior
   ponder my folly full ways
   allow the pounding of my jail-cell conjuring heart to slow, cease

feeling vaguely foolish
as one would

fancy thinking the moon was a cop car
absurd   or so i convinced myself

until at that very moment
the constellation orion
tapped at my window
& politely asked me
to blow
   into a little plastic bag

GLEN JOHNS
Poem of the Month, November 2011

TURNER'S SUNSETS

Turner's adoration of sun & air
his vistas of flaming English skies
his boats tossing on tempestuous seas
his idyllic pastorals & classic marbles
enchanted me long ago

how surprising then to discover
the cause of this golden exuberance
was the violent eruption of Tambora
on the Indonesian Island of Sumbawa
late at night on April 10, 1815.
(Vesuvius was a mere firecracker by comparison)
a cataclysm so violent
that 2000ks away, ash hid China from the sun
corn crops in the US repeatedly failed to grow
& prevented the northern summer

there is something supremely unsettling to think
half a world away in civilisation's heart
no one knew London's sublime sunsets
were caused by light skit-scattering
through megatonnes of volcanic dust
blown high into the atmosphere

particles which would take decades to dissolve
& a lifetime to paint

GLEN JOHNS

MY PIANO

Like the luthier fashioning the wood
so we find this moment
– alone and together
where touch gives rise to conversation
immediate and instinctive
sustained and mellow
loud, angry
soothing, aching
sonorous and sensual

This tryst
this illicit arrangement

Shutting out the clamorous
caustic, shrill voices
the barrage of random sounds
the impertinent imposition
of every assault on our senses

To you, I come
pause – break the silence
sit and play

My piano

GEOFF JOHNSTON

IMAGINING THE MIND OF SOMEONE WHO SEES NO FUTURE FOR REAL BOOKS IN SCHOOLS

The Principal says, 'Laptops are a great tool for students
as it is something they understand.' And
the Principal adds, 'The program would likely see
the school's library books become unnecessary.'
Weekly Times, Messenger Press, 24 November 2010

Didn't her mother read to her each night
let her walk with the walrus and the carpenter
or discover the way of the whirlwind?

Did she never know the intensity of a bushfire
through the tragic story of the death of a wombat or
feel the presence of termites in those magnetic mounds?

Did she never travel upstream with spawning salmon
learn to love the creatures of the wild with Grey Owl
or find in stories of the past truths about our history?

Was there no joy in descriptions of nature study
in the close examination of deft line drawings
of mushrooms and toadstools, stamen and stigma?

Did *Man Must Measure* or *The Ascent of Man* offer
no challenge to go against gravity and climb into
rarified air high above the snow line of Everest?

Did she never pause on a page, find in a line a phrase
to awake the mind to a different approach to a theme
feel the urge to take the time to explore further up stream?

Did she never find in books reasons to laugh or cry, feel
the presence of poverty or pride in other places and want
to engage in the face-to-face learning that might follow?

Is that why she has no time for real books to open minds
and hearts, and has decided to force our youthful future
into the virtual machine-made world away from books?

In her world, her virtual cyber space world
there will be no connections outside of machines,
and one day when the machine stops there'll be …

ERICA JOLLY

READING *BENEATH THE LION'S GAZE* BY MAAZA MENGISTE

Ethopia from 1974 to 1991

I have no need to check batteries
click open or boot up a machine.

I can sit, take in its frightening pages
begin to feel their fear and shake
as I become aware of all their trials.

I can stop, take time to get to know
what refugees from Ethiopia might
have fled – the lucky ones who did escape.

I can pause, go back, stomach churning
to where I left my book mark, face more truth in fiction
without adding a single joule to my power bill.

ERICA JOLLY

FERRY BOAT THROTTLES BACK

Ferry boat throttles back
under a harbour, bridging
goodly vibrations.

KAHLIL JUREIDINI

A TICKET OF LEAVE

A ticket of leave
tickertape of leaves
implosion, autumnal.

KAHLIL JUREIDINI

WILLOW WILLOW

Willow, willow, cricket bat,
Tell me where Ophelia's at??
I've been outside hugging trees
and eating bark where is she please?
They reckon she's around the bend
You think an aspirin would help her mend?
I s'pose I could be wrong I know
O there she floats, going with the flow
Hamlet's wounded name still stings
Weeping willow tears of wood
He draws long bows of cello strings
He once was cheered and now is booed
The willow bends and breaks and falls
And Denmark wins Taswegian belles
Under the weeping willow stands
a man with bat and bow in hands
he hugs the trees and eats the bark
his aspirin breath lights up the dark.

KAHLIL JUREIDINI

DEAR PUBLISHER

Thank you for your offer to publish my poem
however I have decided not to accept
for one or more of the following reasons:

- Your company does not fit my list
- You have published too many poems like my own
- Your company is unmarketable
- Your distribution is limited

- I do not like the poems you have published in the past
- I do not like the colour of your website
- I do not feel you have enough experience
- I do not think your work is of a consistently high standard

However, I do thank you for taking the time
to seek out my poems
and I apologise for the many months
it has taken to get back to you.

Unfortunately my slush pile
of unsolicited publishers
is so deep and so full of dross
it takes great effort to wade through it all.

And, alas, some publishers do not
do their homework well enough
they waste time, theirs and mine,
requesting poems that are clearly unsuitable.

I do wish you luck with your future
publishing endeavours however
and please do not lose heart
it is nothing personal.

Kind regards,

SHARON KERNOT

REMEMBERING THE WORLD

The shadows that were heaped up beneath trees
have left

from between the stoneware
of clouds

the last threads of sunlight
have

fallen

hard

as bits of sunset are flaking off
the high rise apartments

unmanageable length of darkness
has blacked out

suburb after suburb

and now encloses the city
in the tonnage
of night

only the streetlights
and headlights

know exactly what
we cannot remember

of the world.

JULES LEIGH KOCH

THE WOMAN FROM THE SHELTER HOUSE

The woman from the shelter house
lives on the same street

In the playground
her children watch out for bear traps amidst
the climbing ropes
and their sandpit

Behind the breakages of her eyes
her trust and beliefs have been stolen
and the words

That gather along the edge of her mouth
remain unspoken

While the space between her and others
is slammed shut

On the way home her children play
hide and seek
among the street trees

All their escape plans are well rehearsed

JULES LEIGH KOCH
Read at Salisbury, August 2011

SPASMS

A black hole's core is
a place where matter becomes
probability

*

Electrofluid
floating verbs warp, unstable,
exchange each other.

*

Describing atoms,
language can only be used
as in poetry.

*

Noting the item,
not observing the item,
changes the item.

STEPHEN LAWRENCE
Read at RiAus, August 2011

EVERY FEELING

Every feeling
and thought derives from neuro-
chemical events.

A spiritual problem
is a chemical problem.

STEPHEN LAWRENCE
Read at RiAus, August 2011

TIME AND SPACE

Vein-streaked hands
tucked out of sight,
she leans forward,
head tilted just so,
in that position
long perfected
to elicit disclosure.

He's all
knees and elbows
as he gazes,
anywhere but at her eyes,
eager words tumbling
to explain his obsession.

So Gran ...
She stifles a flinch.
The name that conjures love
and pain
in equal parts.

... since the dawn of time ...
She hears,
remembering her dawn,
all that youthful vigour.

... the Universe ...
She sighs.
For her the World
was enough.

... has been expanding ...
She knows too well.
Unfamiliar spaces,
strange contraptions.

And it's still expanding!
Can you imagine the distance?
And she thinks
she almost can.
About as far as the lavatory
at 3 a.m.

KRISTIN MARTIN

WITH A RUSH OF WATER

he reels the fish in,
light glancing off

the tessellation of mirrors
on its wet piscine skin.

In a flash he glimpses his son
writhing in a shawl of amnion,

his wife begging for oxygen
in her river of blood.

He unhooks the pleading mouth,
spills the fish over the bank

where the current swallows it
like a bolus of grief.

Beneath the meniscus
of his breathing world

the barb still hangs,
trails the air.

LOUISE McKENNA

CHOCOLATE WATTLED BAT
Chalinolobus morio

Settling into bed with a book
the silence is electrified
there is another presence in the room

in a flash of negative lightning
black bolt against the light
the bat banks and vanishes

I search corners and corners
and again it flashes with only the sound
of slipping past air and air not noticing

it pauses, scouring this branchless wasteland
trepidatious ears frantically swivelling
for the familiar tunes of wind and kin

head hunkered into the neck's deep ruff
the fine-boned leather arcs against the light
in Teflon navigation of this blind sky

Door open, it senses the known and is gone
swiftly shuttling the fine threads of dark
weaving the silence with pulse and echo.

RACHAEL MEAD
Mentored poet 2011
Poem of the Month, March 2011

THE STORM

clouds held afternoon sun under blind stars
all day isobars tumbling together
drew the sinew from our limbs
the first wave blew us into bed

the wind, lost in the steep maze of valleys, panicked
thrashing around the house as if caught in a net
forcing its fingers under the gutters, trying to peer in
as if we held the secret to escape

gum nuts hailed onto tin in staccato bursts
snare drum counterpoint to the woodwind howl
all night we waited for the birds
to peal the all clear

at dawn we emerged to a shuffled world
the blue spruce parasol missing a rib
and the road under the stringybarks now a soft forest path
strewn with the wild prunings of the storm gardener

RACHAEL MEAD
Mentored poet 2011

SUMMER BRONZEWINGS

Upon viewing Bronzewings and Saplings *Hans Heysen 1921*

Sun has stripped crisp bark
from skinny-dipping saplings
bathing in mid-morning glow

As turkeys strut and scatter litter
helter-skelter, scarcely seeing
your easel, your satisfied smile.

Exuberant in their love of life
resplendent in their feathered finery,
they gobble-gossip loudly while they work.

Deftly you paint a complex pattern,
column and arc, column and arc,
show-off fans of white and bronze.

Burnished blue on wings and blue on foliage,
red and bronze of wrinkled head and peeling bark
among the youthful sheen of saplings.

Clear light, warmth and harmony,
painted with a sure and steady hand.
Watercolour perfection, Hans.

JACQUI MERCKENSCHLAGER

CHANNELLED ENERGY

Jump in back, you kids
    up in back o' ute, under tarp.
Quiet now,   like little
tadpoles – no, not wrigglers!
Police might catch us.
Too many tadpoles,
    no seat belts.

OK,   all out!
Here – take them strings and bait.
Watch us catch them
yabbies in channel
    Wall Flat channel.
Now you kids!

Jimmy, you got some?
Yeahs, three.   But need thirteen.
Promised thirteen old ladies.
Yabbies been ordered.
Saving biggest but
for my grandmother!

You kids done all right
today.   Better than
makin' trouble in town, ana?
Trouble is,   gove'nment filling
them channels soon.
No yabbies then, eh kids?

MAX MERCKENSCHLAGER
Read at Salisbury, August 2011
Poem of the Month, September 2011

HOLIDAY

the west coast of irish light
is inside everything and through everything
like the washing on the line, the pegs
the sky, the wind, this window, and your hands, your eyes
the yolk of daisies and the white
stone walls of cottages with slate roofs
clipped with strips of tin, and rooks and crows
gulls and blackbirds, sheep and cows all caught in the same spell
from before morning until after night
for eighteen hours a day the photons
scooped off the atlantic and smashed into peat bogs, earth,
    fence-wire, rust, paint
bushes, mountains, cars and roads and poems
to borrow a licence from wright
build for their own resurrection day
in a one-way experiment with wild geese, swans, the coil of air,
    and cold
and rain five minutes ago, and in five minutes' time, rain
compacted with second sight
hedges and ditches, smoke, thought, clouds and mist compressed,
    compelled
annealed and overlaid, and overloaded with clarity, clamped down
into landscape already magnified with force, worn inward and set,
    against the horizon
steeped in a paradox of height
confined to mid-range, revealed at human scale, condensed,
    but unabridged, unabbreviated
the quality of illumination is absolute, intensified, unshielded,
    unchallenged, understated
quiet, like the moon lit from within, rock, bone, a candle,
    a teardrop, enamelled and sprung, sheer
and supersaturated deep bright

DAVID MORTIMER

VIETNAM

The letter came:
he failed the medical.
Lizzie and Dianne whooped and cheered
and Ian and Maggie waltzed on the lawn
Father went into the shed
for a quiet moment
and joy, like a blast of helium,
filled Mother's balloon heart.
She clapped along as they dipped and swayed
the only ballast holding her down
the thought of that other woman
whose son would go instead.

MARIANNE MUSGROVE

TO SOAR
for Dorothy McKay

Here on the heights
of Stanwell Park, rugged up
against the eager breeze
that skips over the waves
far below, braces itself
for the sudden climb
then leaps up over the edge
of the cliff like a puppy
looking for someone to play with,

I recognise you in the woman
who starts down the slope
then is suddenly afloat
on the fathomless air,
playing chasey with the currents,
making sweeping turns in search of
updrafts' hidden pathways,
the kite's knife-edge slicing smoothly
through the sky's transparent waves.

It's here that I see you,
not in your hospice bed,
but spiralling in the lively air,
dancing with stately grace
in the arms of the spirited wind,
nursed by the earth's breath,
soaring the thermals
like a white-breasted sea-eagle
on upswept wings.

JOHN PFITZNER
Poem of the Month, October 2011

POINTLESS

for Graham, who is mad on sport
but sees no use for poetry

You're right, there's no point
to poetry. It's as useless

as a Michael Clarke cover drive
with dancing foot work,
body balanced, head steady,
weight gliding to the front foot,
the almost lazy sweep of the bat,
the perfect timing and rhythm,
the flow of the follow-through,
the seemingly effortless elegance,

which changes nothing, adds nothing
to the sum of human knowledge,
rights no wrongs, cures no diseases,
provides no food for the starving,

as pointless as a poem
with language that dances down the pitch,
gives itself room and launches
its outrageous idea, its subtle
observation high over midwicket
and into the members stand
with perfect timing, rhythm and
seemingly effortless eloquence.

JOHN PFITZNER

TO KEVIN

Meanwhile,
you wrote your first poem,

cramped like children's scissors
in an adult hand.

The same day you bought a vanilla bean –
just to smell it –

and a single olive to eat.

Counting each sweet thing
to your store:

a woman's skirt
flowering around her,

a child letting go
of a sole balloon.

the salted sweat
running down your lover's breast.

How quietly you kissed her,
bearing verses in your mind.

CLAIRE M. ROBERTS

GLACIER

Ice crawls thick
heavy and slow
deep crevices hold air
with a frozen peace
aimed at silent suffocation
holding secrets and rocks
from centuries past
kept bound in white
there's no innocence here
tinges of blue suck life away
a power grinds
down the mountain
death creeps and steals
until ice softens
in thunderous protest
as carving drops pieces
to form lakes and rivers
for the living to drink.

LILLIANA ROSE

SOUP OR NOT

She is like God
the way she watches you
turn yourself inside out to question question
and bounce it straight back at you.
She presides in her high chair
over the array of food presented;
tasting nothing, she spreads it around,
stirs the brown gravy green peas and white potato
into a marbled mash
till it becomes a dull grey,
all with a cool detachment.
After hammering with questions
you offer a bowl of noodle soup –
noodles are irresistible to children –
asking **do you want soup or not**
before you risk leaving it.
She looks you square in the face
and with blue bland eyes says
Soupornot

ROS SCHULZ

COULD WE *PLEASE* GET BACK TO LINEAR?

kids' reading levels are falling off

no wonder   there aren't any

levels

I mean

in every school text

be it hi

story   or science   just   **balloooooons** of instructions

I need   a list   a sequence   that tells me

how to do ONE   before I do TWO

and I'm   given   **ballooooons** of text   and asked to

leap like batman   from the top of a chimney

scale a building like phantom   to fit together A and B

sure I read comics   way back

I could fly like Superman   from one height

to another   make sense of

the sudden miraculous appearance   in a weird position

of a rescuing hero

but

not

here

trying to span a river
one rock at a time
without falling in.

ROS SCHULZ

LITTLE ANGEL

He resembles some perfect Jesus chipped from a marble
    masterpiece:
he is too beautiful.
For, me, I am a devil for the smoke.
He has tumbled into the smoky hell, which I know too well.
Which will render him grey as this ashen layette I've fashioned
    for him.
As long as I am smoking I wish I were not.
Even if I am only deserving of the worst, remember this incongruity:
This little angel awaits me.
Let my heart, my mind, my breath in-kind be as
sweet as the milk my body makes him.
He deserves to taste and hear and see
the unexpected best
of a better me.

A.M. SLADDIN

STROLLING ALONG

Just when I've grudgingly cleaned the stroller,
washed the lambskin and
Father has sewn the harness shorter to fit him in
after a feverish trip "round the cabin"
I consider the marathon of touring the block
still silently cursing my fulfilled wish
when I see this:
an old-lady tramp her pusher piled high with
drink cans and hard rubbish
and I see that other, lonely, me
that I do no longer want to be
and
instead, put him in;
and we go for a stroll
me sporting again freedom's rare grin.

A.M. SLADDIN

I COULD LIVE

In a motel room forever
black pen white paper
red wine
as long as outside
was always different
I like the outside to change

This week a long jetty, fishing boats
one day a river with weeping willows
next week eucalypt, saltbush, mallee
then on to red sand and blue space
next month old churches and cemeteries

As for inside, I don't care
I could live in a motel room
if the door always opened
to new worlds
if the door always closed

on conventions
left me with pen paper wine
and time
I could live.

J.A. STEELE

HAY CUTTING

Brown hills shave back
to corduroy
in the final hour of light.

On the hill-line a tractor
rumouring on –
riding a wave of grass,

skirting the knuckles of quartz
that punch up
through the clay.

It comes and goes
through nightfall –
a blazing-white, low star.

THOM SULLIVAN

MORNING RAIN IN THE MacCULLOCHS

You sleep – and while you sleep
the rain comes on:
gentle at first,
then rising like applause
across the iron roof.
Beads of water penetrate the flywire,
studding your socks
like glass;
stippling the magazine
upturned on your knees.
Timber boards secrete
a heady stench of dust –
earth-scent infused
with the pungency of rain.
Beyond the verandah's low horizon,
a bruised sky –
lightning shivering
across an underbelly of cloud.

THOM SULLIVAN

WIPEOUT

It's obvious
i can see it in your eyes
watercolour seascapes
moving the tides
you could paint the moment
beyond memory
so that I forget
where I was
before you

JENNY TOUNE

WAITING

A crease of light, a crack, a minute sliver
of gold that cut the darkness like a knife.
She hunched herself against the sight,
and drew the blankets closer round her neck.
Perhaps if she was very quiet, shut her eyes,
it might not widen, open, allow the dangers
of the night their entry. A moment's darkness –
relief, release of breath she had been holding.
But no, a mere illusion of reprieve; the door
swung open, sharp with menace. He came in.

VALERIE VOLK

POSTCARDS

Soft option – isn't it? A postcard, when you can't think
what to write. But then, it poses its own problems.
What to say? "I'm having a great time!" is almost
like a two-edged sword to those you've left behind …
And also hypocritical, those phrases of convention:
"Wish that you were here." Then what is left to use?
Stray social comments on the weather, or the scenery?
"Snowed last night" is scarcely relevant, when those at home
are sweltering in bushfire heat. Perhaps I'll leave my efforts,
only add, just as dishonestly, "With love."

VALERIE VOLK

ODE TO TRACEY

inspired by Catullus Poem 6

After visiting the Saatchi exhibition at the SA Art Gallery.
For further enlightenment, Google 'Tracey's Bed'.

O Tracey, why do you flaunt your love!
I first met you stitching patiently for hours
embroidering the names of all the lovers
that shared your deepest secrets
men, women, even your own mother
filled your tiny nomad's tent
with signatures of passing ardour
that has long since cooled or wandered on.
How I longed to be part of
your private world, to have my name
forever immortalised in the weave
of your strange and fragile universe.
But now you whip the covering away
displaying your naked bed for all to see
laying bare your sordid habits
the sheets still warm and soiled with passion's juice
our final night of amorous dalliance
exposed like an altar to the public eye.
Ah! Woe the day I sought to woo you
thinking a poet could capture an artist's heart
I little thought I would become a mere component
in an installation devoted entirely to the ego.

Alas! You have sacrificed our precious intimacy
to the grand, gross goddess of crass celebrity.

JULIA WAKEFIELD

IN JAPAN

In Japan
they line up
to be hugged
by a machine

G.M. WALKER

SLUGGISH RETURNS

The dew dragged that giant slug from

the retaining wall again last night

Perhaps he was indecisive

on the up/down question

Perhaps he has a one-second memory

and constructs his journeys randomly

Perhaps he was lost

Perhaps he just wanted to leave me

a silvered graph of yesterday's

All Ordinaries Index

ROB WALKER
Poem of the Month, January 2011

CLOZE PROCEDURE

we are at the zoo when
your doctor calls you

talk about the lump i
fill gaps from a half

conversation sun beats
on our bare heads   i

think of cancer nervous
meerkats sit up take

notice as you ask a
phone do I need an

ultrasound   we all turn
heads inquisitively

awaiting an answer

ROB WALKER

CHEMISTRY

Oxygen Deuterium electron
Tritium Oxygen
Sulphur Tellurium Tungsten

Sulphur Tellurium Tungsten Argon Tritium
Tungsten Arsenic   Oxygen Neon
Scandium Iodine electron Nitrogen Tritium Iodine
Sulphur Tritium,
Boron Uranium Tritium,   Aluminium Arsenic,   Helium
Iodine Sulphur   Nobelium   Molybdenum Rhenium,
Beryllium Carbon Gold Selenium
Tungsten Hydrogen Astatine   Helium
Deuterium Radium Nitrogen Potassium Arsenic H_2O,
Tungsten Arsenic H_2SO_4

STEWART WALKER

TRANSLATION

$^{16}O^2De^-$
$^3T^{16}O$
$^{34}S^{127}Te^{184}W$

$^{34}S^{128}Te^{184}W^{40}Ar^3T$ $^{184}W^{75}As$ $^{16}O^{20}Ne$
$^{45}Sc^{127}Ie^{-14}N^3T^{127}I^{34}S^3T$,
$^{11}B^{238}U^3T$ $^{27}Al^{75}As$ ^4He
$^{127}I^{34}S$ ^{254}No $^{96}Mo^{186}Re$,
$^9Be^{12}C^{197}Au^{79}Se$ $^{184}W^1H^{210}At$ ^4He
$^2D^{226}Ra^{14}N^{39}K$ ^{75}As $^1H_2^{16}O$,
$^{184}W^{75}As$ $^1H_2^{34}S^{16}O_4$.

^{32}S ^{128}Te ^{184}W ^{40}Ar ^3T ^{184}W ^{27}Al ^{39}K ^{167}Er —
ELEMENTARY SPELLING

WE DISCUSSED TEA AND THE UNIVERSE

I wanted to ask you for your chai recipe,
It sounded delicious;
The thought taste of ginger and cinnamon
and what was it? Citrus? Pepper?

I wanted to ask you because I forgot
to write it down, like the lines of a poem
that drop into my lap
while I'm driving.

I wanted to ask you for your chai recipe
because you loved it so much;
but I forgot.
So I will drink my own tea.

I will savour the richness of taste,
thoughts and memories of a friend
whose chai recipe, like her smile,
is no more.

SARAH WAUCHOPE

GO BLIND AND EASY INTO THAT FINAL LEAP

(A Poem on dying well. A response to Dylan Thomas)

Go blind and easy into that final leap.
Death, slide into sheets like a lover
with no sore secrets left on lips to steep.
Wise women know the final path is steep
No stage required to be a crossed lover,
so go blind and easy into that final leap.
Good women, the last bed made, weave to sleep
silk threads of their grief, to cover,
with no soul secrets left on lips to steep.
Wild women that drank the blue songs of the deep
learn through to the end, love spills over,
so go blind and easy into that final leap.
Grave poets may let cold fears speak
and stain a life like an absent mother,
with still sore secrets left on lips to keep.
You, my sister, your ticket to the deep,
kiss and smile, wish me the same ride over
Go blind and easy into that final leap
with no sad secrets left on lips to keep.

CARMEL WILLIAMS

FIRST LIGHT
to Lachlan

In that black hell of hot, humid jungle
The signal –
Confirmed.

Attack first light –
0545 hours
Nam time.

Like machinegun parts worn too thin,
Men,
Wishing to survive,
With dimmed torches
Double checked their best friend,
Their SLR,
Then fixed sharpened and oiled bayonets.

The ammo and grenade pouches checked
Those with M60 ammo belts
Slung them around their overloaded shoulders

The section moved off.

The bloody jungle waiting for first light.

GEORGE WOOLMER
Poem of the Month, April 2011

For further information about
Friendly Street publications and activities please visit
our website: friendlystreetpoets.org.au
email: poetry@friendlystreetpoets.org.au
postal: PO Box 3697, Norwood SA 5067

§